جيتار الحُبّ

كتبْها مُحمّد صُبْحي

The Guitar of Love

Egyptian Arabic Reader – Book 3

by Mohamed Sobhy

lingualism

ISBN: 978-1-949650-13-6

Written by Mohamed Sobhy

Edited by Matthew Aldrich

Cover art by Duc-Minh Vu

Audio by Heba Salah Ali

website: www.lingualism.com

email: contact@lingualism.com

Introduction

The **Egyptian Arabic Readers** series aims to provide learners with much-needed exposure to authentic language. The books in the series are at a similar level (B1-B2) and can be read in any order. The stories are a fun and flexible tool for building vocabulary, improving language skills, and developing overall fluency.

The main text is presented on even-numbered pages with tashkeel (diacritics) to aid in reading, while parallel English translations on odd-numbered pages are there to help you better understand new words and idioms. A second version of the text is given at the back of the book, without the distraction of tashkeel and translations, for those who are up to the challenge.

New to this edition: the English translations have been revised for improved clarity and accuracy. Each story now also includes **20 comprehension questions** with example answers to help reinforce your understanding of the text. A **sequencing exercise** is provided as well, where you'll put ten key events from the story back in their correct order. These additions make the book even more useful for self-study, classroom use, or group discussions.

Visit www.lingualism.com/audio, to stream or download the free accompanying audio.

This book is also available in Modern Standard Arabic at www.lingualism.com/msar.

جيتار الحُبّ

أُتوبيس المَدْرسة مِسْتنّي علاء، دايْماً آخِر واحِد بِيرْكِب الأُتوبيس لإنُّه أقْرب واحِد لِلمدْرسة.

نِزِل علاء مِن بيْتُه و رِكِب الأُتوبيس. و دايْماً بِيْحِبّ يُقْعُد على الجنْب اليِمين علشان يِبُصّ على رنا اللي دايْماً بِتُقْعُد وَرا سوّاق الأُتوبيس في الشِّمال.

و فِضِل علاء ساكِت و هادي، و كُلّ التّلاميذ بِيعْمِلوا دَوْشة في الأُتوبيس... حتّى سوّاق الأُتوبيس أوْقات بِيِتْضايِق و يقولُّهُم: "ما كِفايَة بقى! بلاش الصّوْت العالي. أنا راسي وَجعِتْني!"

لمّا الأُتوبيس وصِل لِلمدْرسة، و نِزِل علاء، لِقي أحْمد بِيجْري عليْه.

"علاء! أخيراً جيت. أنا كُنْت مِسْتنّيك!"

علاء قال: "ليْه بسّ؟ فيه أيْه؟"

أحْمد ردّ: "معْلِشّ بسّ أنا تعْبان و مِش قادِر... كحّ كحّ!"

"ألْف سلامة!"

"لأ لأ لأ، ألْف سلامة أيْه بسّ؟ المفْروض أنا في الإذاعة المدْرسية. و أنا تعْبان و مِش قادِر... كحّ كحّ!"

The school bus is waiting for Alaa, who's always the last one to get on because he lives closest to the school.

Alaa came out of his house and got on the bus. He always likes to sit on the right side so he can look at Rana, who always sits behind the bus driver on the left.

Alaa stayed quiet and calm, while all the students were making noise on the bus... even the bus driver sometimes gets annoyed and says to them, "That's enough already! No more loud noise. I've got a headache!"

When the bus arrived at school and Alaa got off, he saw Ahmad running toward him.

"Alaaa! You finally came. I was waiting for you!"

Alaa said, "Why though? What's going on?"

Ahmad replied, "Sorry, but I'm sick and I can't... cough, cough!"

"Get well soon!"

"No, no, no—get well soon, what? I'm supposed to be on the school broadcast. But I'm sick and I can't... cough, cough!"

"أنا عُمْري ما طِلِعْت الإذاعة المدْرسية، و خايِف أغْلط."

"لأ لأ لأ، مِش هتِغْلط، متْخافْش."

أحْمد نادى بِصوْت عالي: "خلاص يا أُسْتاذ فهْمي... علاء هَيِطْلع مكاني!"

"بسّ أنا مقُلْتِش إنّ هطْلع."

أحْمد قال: "خلاص بقى، خلّيك جدع معايا[1]!"

الأُسْتاذ فهْمي راح لعلاء و قالُه: "يَلّا يا علاء! هتِقْرا الأخْبار الصّباحية، و خلّي صوْتك هادي و متِقْراش بِسُرْعة."

علاء ردّ: "بسّ أنا..."

الأُسْتاذ فهْمي بِصوْت عالي زعّ: "يَلّا كُلُّه على طابورُه[2]!"

وقِف علاء ماسِك الجُرْنال و بدأ يِقرا الخبر بيْنُه و بيْن نفْسُه علشان مَيِتْلخْبطْش.

و علاء اتْوَتّر و بدأ يِعْرق.

و أحْمد واقِف في طابور فصْلُه و قاعِد يِضْحك معَ صُحابُه.

علاء قال لنفْسُه: "مُسْتحيل أحْمد يِكون تعْبان. تعْبان و هَيِضْحك و يِلْعب كِده إزّاي!؟"

Audio Track Timestamp: [1:30]

"I've never done the school broadcast before, and I'm scared I'll mess up."

"No, no, no, you won't mess up. Don't worry."

Ahmad called out loudly: "That's it, Mr. Fahmi... Alaa will go up instead of me!"

"But I didn't say I would go."

Ahmad said, "Come on now, be a good friend to me!"

Mr. Fahmi went to Alaa and said, "Come on, Alaa! You'll read the morning news—keep your voice calm and don't read too fast."

Alaa replied, "But I..."

Mr. Fahmi shouted loudly, "Everyone, get in your lines!"

Alaa stood holding the newspaper and started reading the news to himself so he wouldn't mess up.

Alaa got nervous and started to sweat.

Meanwhile, Ahmad was standing in his class line laughing with his friends.

Alaa said to himself, "No way Ahmad is sick. Sick and laughing and playing like that?!"

---

[1] خلّيك جدع معايا lit. *be good with me, that is, be a pal*

[2] The school day in Egypt starts with طابور المدْرسة (lit. *school line-up*), a morning assembly.

تِلْميذ نادى مِن بعيد: "أُسْتاذ فَهْمي! أُسْتاذ فَهْمي! المايْكْرُفُوْن مِش شغّال!"

أُسْتاذ فَهْمي قال: "يَعْني أيْه مِش شغّال؟"

بدأت أصوات التّلاميذ في الطّابور تِعْلى و بدأ الضّحْك و الهِزار. و الأُسْتاذ فَهْمي فِضِل يِحاوِل يِصلّح المايْكْرُفُوْن.

الأُسْتاذ فَهْمي قال بِصوْت عالي: "خلاص دِلْوَقْتي! اِطْلعوا لِلْفُصول."

علاء حطّ الجُرْنال على الطّرابيْزة،. و طِلع مَعَ أصحابُه لِلْفصْل و هُوَّ مِتْنرْفِز.

لكِنِ الأُسْتاذ فَهْمي وَقّفه. "إنت مرْعوب كِده ليْه؟ خايِف مِن شُوَيّةٌ كلام هتْقولُهُم في المايْكْرُفُوْن؟"

علاء ردّ: "هُوَّ أنا بسّ..."

"اِطْلع خلاص، أنا بنْصحك[1]!"

طِلع علاء لِلْفصْل و هُوَّ مِتْضايِق و شاف أحْمد.

علاء زعّق لِأحْمد و قال: "مكانْش يِنْفع تِعْمِل اللي إنْتَ عملْتُه ده على فِكْرة!"

"يا عمّ خلاص بقى محصلْش حاجة."

[2:49]

A student called from afar: "Mr. Fahmi! Mr. Fahmi! The microphone's not working!"

Mr. Fahmi said, "What do you mean it's not working?"

The students in the lineup started raising their voices, and laughter and joking began. Mr. Fahmi kept trying to fix the microphone.

Mr. Fahmi shouted loudly, "That's it for now! Go to your classes."

Alaa put the newspaper on the table and went to class with his friends, annoyed.

But Mr. Fahmi stopped him. "Why are you so scared? You're afraid of a few words you were going to say into the microphone?"

Alaa replied, "It's just that I..."

"Just go now, that's my advice!"

Alaa went to class, upset, and saw Ahmad.

Alaa shouted at Ahmad and said, "You really shouldn't have done what you did, by the way!"

"Come on, man, nothing happened."

---

[1] بِنْصَحَك lit. *I'm advising you, that is, it'd be best for you if you...*

"لأ حصل! إنْتَ خلّيتْني مِتْضايِق دِلْوَقْتي."

دخل المُدرِّس على التّلاميذ و قالُهُم: "سُكوت! سُكوت!"

و بعْدَيْن كمّل: "بِما إنّي جِديد هِنا، فا عرّفوني بيكُم يا شباب! أنا أُستاذ اللُّغة العربية و إنّ شاء اللّه يِكون درْس مُمْتع لِيكو. النّهارْده مِش هناخُد حاجات كِتير. كُلّ واحِد بسّ يِكْتِب بَياناتُه في ورْقة علشان أقْدر أتْواصل معَ أهْلُكو دايْماً!"

الطُّلّاب كتبوا البَيانات: الإسْم، رقم التِّليفوْن، و رقم الفصْل.

علاء كان دايْماً بِيُقْعُد في أوّل كُرْسي. و علشان كِده المُدرِّس قالُه يِلِمّ الورَق و يِودّيهولُه على المكْتب.

علاء كان بِيلِمّ الورَق مِن الطُّلّاب... و لمّا خد الورْقة بِتاعِةْ رنا، خلّى الورْقة بِتاعِتْها آخِر ورْقة.

و بعْد ما لمّ كُلّ الورَق، و هُوَّ رايِح للمُدرِّس، شاف ورْقِةْ رنا. و فِضِل يِردِّد رقم التِّليفوْن كإنّه بِيردِّد الأخْبار بِتاعِةْ الجُرْنال بالظّبْط.

بعْد ما وَصّل الورَق للمُدرِّس، راح الحمّام و كتب بِسُرْعة على إيدُه رقم رنا. بسّ مِن تحْت كُمّ القميص اللي كان لابْسُه عشان محدِّش بِشوفُه.

و لمّا طِلِع علاء مِن الحمّام، شاف الأُسْتاذ فهْمي.

[4:10]

"No, something did happen! You made me upset now."

The teacher came into the classroom and said to the students, "Silence! Silence!"

Then he continued, "Since I'm new here, introduce yourselves, guys! I'm the Arabic teacher, and God willing, it'll be a fun class for you. Today, we're not going to cover much. Each of you just write your information on a piece of paper so I can always stay in touch with your families!"

The students wrote down their info: name, phone number, and class number.

Alaa always sat in the first seat, so the teacher told him to collect the papers and bring them to his desk.

Alaa was collecting the papers from the students... and when he took Rana's paper, he made sure hers was the last one.

After collecting all the papers, while heading toward the teacher, he looked at Rana's paper and kept repeating her phone number as if he were reciting the news from the newspaper exactly.

After delivering the papers to the teacher, he went to the bathroom and quickly wrote Rana's number on his hand—but under the sleeve of the shirt he was wearing so no one would see it.

When Alaa came out of the bathroom, he saw Mr. Fahmi.

علاء قال: "يا أُسْتاذ فهْمي، مُمْكِن تِدّيني فُرْصة أَثْبِتْلك إنّي شُجاع؟"

الأُسْتاذ فهْمي ردّ و قال: "الإثْبات هُوَّ إثْبات لِنفْسك، مِش لِيّا!"

"طيِّب، مُمْكِن أعْزِف بُكْره في طابور المدْرسة... بِالجِّيتار بِتاعي؟"

"ماشي، و مِتْخافْش تاني بعْد كِده!"

◆   ◆   ◆

بعْد أوِّل يوْم دِراسي، رِجِع علاء في الأُتوبيس... و لِإنُّه آخِر واحِد بيِرْكب الأُتوبيس، إلّا إنُّه أوِّل واحِد بيِنْزِل مِن الأُتوبيس.

علاء قال لِنفْسُه و هُوَّ باصِص على رنا: "مكْتوب عليّا أشوفِك دقايِق قبْل ما أنْزِل و دقايِق بعْد ما أرْكب. لوْ كان في إيدي، كُنْت هخلّيكي قُدّامي كِده ٢٤ ساعة!"

رنا كانِت مُتَوَسِّطِةْ الجمال. على غيْر المُتَوَقّع علاء كمان كان مُتَوَسِّط الجمال، لكِنُّه كان شايِف إنّ رنا أجْمل بِنْت في الفصْل كُلّه.

نِزِل علاء مِن الأُتوبيس و رِجِع البيْت.

لمّا رِجِع علاء البيْت و بعْد ساعات، اتِّصل على رقم رنا.

[5:55]

Alaa said, "Mr. Fahmi, can you give me a chance to prove to you that I'm brave?"

Mr. Fahmi replied, "Proving it is for yourself, not for me!"

"Okay, can I play my guitar tomorrow during the school lineup?"

"Alright, and don't be afraid again after this!"

❖ ❖ ❖

After the first day of school, Alaa rode home on the bus… and since he's the last one to get on the bus, that means he's the first to get off.

Alaa said to himself as he looked at Rana, "It's my fate to see you just for a few minutes before I get off and a few minutes after I get on. If it were up to me, I'd have you in front of me like this 24 hours a day!"

Rana was moderately beautiful. Surprisingly, Alaa was also moderately handsome, but he thought Rana was the most beautiful girl in the whole class.

Alaa got off the bus and went home.

When Alaa got home and after a few hours, he called Rana's number.

و قلْب علاء بِيُنْبُض بِقُوّة و بِيتْحرّك مِن مكانُه... لِحدّ ما رنا ردِّت: "ألوْ؟"

علاء حطّ إيدُه على بُقُّه عشان صوْتُه مَيطْلعْش. و فِضِل يِسْمع رنا و هِيَّ بِتْقول: "ألو؟ ألوْ؟" لِحدّ ما قفلِت المُكالْمة.

دخل علاء أوْضْتُه و هُوَّ مبْسوط، و جاب الجيتار بِتاعُه، و قفل باب الأوْضة، و قعد يِعْزِف و يُرْقُص بِالجِّيتار بِتاعُه. "ألوْ! ألوْ! ألووووْ! ألوْ!"

و كتب رقم رنا على ضهْر الجيتار و رسم جنْبُه قلْب و حطّ الجيتار جنْبُه على السِّرير.

❖   ❖   ❖

تاني يوْم راح علاء بِسُرْعة و جاب الجيتار اللي في أوْضِةْ الموسيقى و جهِّز نفْسُه قبْل الطّابور كُلُّه ما يِبْدأ.

الأُسْتاذ فهْمي بصّ لِعلاء و قالُه: "جاهِز يا علاء؟"

علاء شاوِر بِراسُه لتحْت: "أَيْوَه."

و لمّا بدأ الطّابور و بدأ علاء العزْف، بدأ واثِق مِن نفْسُه لكنُّه بصّ لِرنا في الطّابور.

و حسّ إنُّه بدأ يِتْلخْبط. و بعْد عشر دقايِق حسّ إنّ أصوات كلام التّلاميذ أعْلى مِن صوْت العزْف بِتاعُه.

[7:20]

Alaa's heart was pounding and beating out of his chest... until Rana answered: "Hello?"

Alaa put his hand over his mouth so his voice wouldn't come out. He just kept listening to Rana saying: "Hello? Hello?" until she hung up.

Alaa went into his room feeling happy, grabbed his guitar, closed the door, and started playing and dancing with his guitar. "Hello! Hello! Helloooo! Hello!"

He wrote Rana's number on the back of the guitar, drew a heart next to it, and placed the guitar beside him on the bed.

❖   ❖   ❖

The next day, Alaa rushed in and got the guitar from the music room and got himself ready before the whole school assembly started.

Mr. Fahmi looked at Alaa and said, "Ready, Alaa?"

Alaa nodded his head down: "Yeah."

When the lineup started and Alaa began playing, he started out confident, but he looked at Rana in the lineup.

And he felt like he was starting to mess up. After ten minutes, he felt like the students' chatter was louder than his playing.

و بصّ لِرنا تاني و اتْوتّر أكْتر و قام فجْأه و وقّف عزْف.

و التّلاميذ ضِحكوا بِصوْت عالي و أوّلُهُم أحْمد. و الأُسْتاذ فهْمي قال بِصوْت مِتنرْفِز: "اِطْلعوا لِلفصْل!"

❖ ❖ ❖

التّلاميذ و هُمّا داخْلين الفصْل فضْلوا يِضْحكوا.

أحْمد قال لِعلاء بِترْيَقة: "أيْه العزْف ده كُلُّه يا فنّان؟"

علاء ردّ: "إنِّي أعْزِف وِحش أحْسن مِن إنّك مبْتِعْزِفْش خالِص على فِكْرة." قام مِشي أحْمد.

فِضِل علاء باصِص ناحْيِةْ البنات... لِرنا بمعْنى أصحّ.

المُدرِّس دخل و بصّ علاء لِلمُدرِّس، و كُلّ مرّة المُدرِّس يِكْتِب على السّبّورة، يِسْتغِلّ علاء اللّحظات دي في إنُّه يبُصّ لِرنا. مِسْتنّي مِنْها تِبُصّله مرّة واحْدة، و لوْ بِالصُّدْفة.

المُدرِّس بصّ لِلتّلاميذ و قالُهُم: "درْس النّهارْده عن العطاء!"

و بعْد شرْح كِتير خِلِص الدّرْس، و خِلِصت كُلّ الدُّروس و التّلاميذ رِجْعوا لِلبيْت. و رِجِع علاء لِلبيْت و فِضِل يِتّصِل تاني و تاني بِرنا. عشان بسّ يِسْمع "ألوْ؟" و أحْياناً "مين معايا؟"

[8:54]

He looked at Rana again, got more nervous, and suddenly stopped playing.

The students burst into loud laughter, led by Ahmad. Mr. Fahmi said in an irritated voice, "Go to your classes!"

❖   ❖   ❖

As the students walked into class, they kept laughing.

Ahmad said to Alaa sarcastically, "What was that performance, maestro?"

Alaa replied, "Playing badly is better than not playing at all, just so you know." Ahmad walked away.

Alaa kept glancing toward the girls... or more precisely, at Rana.

The teacher came in, and every time he wrote on the board, Alaa used those moments to sneak looks at Rana—just hoping she'd look at him once, even by accident.

The teacher looked at the students and said, "Today's lesson is about giving!"

After a long explanation, the lesson ended, all the classes ended, and the students went home. Alaa got home and kept calling Rana again and again—just to hear "Hello?" and sometimes, "Who's this?"

أبو علاء دخل على علاء الأوْضة، قام علاء قافِل التِّليفوْن بِسُرْعة.

أبو علاء قال: "بِيْقولوا فيه رِحْلة لِلصّحرا معَ المدْرسة. عايِز تِروح؟"

"لأ بلاش. هِنا أحْسن مِن الصّحرا. و بعْديْن فيه رِحْلة لِلإسْتاد مُمْكِن أروحْها معَ صُحابي."

"خلاص ماشي، شوف إنْتَ عايِز أيْه."

جرس التِّليفوْن رنّ.

أبو علاء قال: "روح بقى رُدّ بِسُرْعة. تِلاقيهُمْ ¹ أصْحابك."

ردّ علاء على التِّليفوْن، و قال: "ألوْ، مين معايا؟"

"أنا صاحْبك يا عمرّ. قول بسّ، هتيجي معانا الإسْتاد و نِشوف ماتْش كوْرة وَلّا تِروح رِحْلةِ الصّحرا معَ البنات؟"

"هُوَّ كُلّ اللي رايِح الصّحرا بنات بسّ يَعْني؟"

واحِد تاني مِن الصُّحاب قال: "ههههههه لأ لأ. بسّ عشان إحْنا رِجالة نِروح أحْسن الإسْتاد."

"أنا قُلْت لِبابا فِعْلاً بلاش فِكْرِةْ الصّحرا دي."

واحِد مِن صُحاب علاء قال: "خلاص اتّفقْنا. الإسْتاد إنّ شاء اللّه!"

[10:26]

Alaa's father came into the room, and Alaa quickly hung up the phone.

Alaa's father said, "They say there's a school trip to the desert. Want to go?"

"Nah, better not. Here is better than the desert. Besides, there's a trip to the stadium I might go on with my friends."

"Alright, whatever you want."

The phone rang.

Alaa's father said, "Go on, answer it quick. It's probably your friends."

Alaa answered the phone and said, "Hello, who's this?"

"It's your buddy, man. Just tell me—are you coming with us to the stadium to watch the football match, or are you going on the desert trip with the girls?"

"So you're saying everyone going to the desert is girls only?"

Another friend said, "Hahaha, no, no. But since we're men, it's better we go to the stadium."

"I already told my dad I'd skip the whole desert idea."

One of Alaa's friends said, "Alright then, it's settled. The stadium, God willing!"

---

[1] تِلاقيهُم lit. *you will find them [to be]*

❖ ❖ ❖

بعْدها بِيوم علاء راح لِمُشْرِف الرِّحلات.

علاء سأل: "لَوْ سمحْت يا أُسْتاذ، أنا عايِز أروح الرِّحْلِتين. الإسْتاد و الصَّحرا. مُمْكِن؟"

المُدرِّس ردّ: "ماشي بسّ كِده هَيْكون غالي عليْك."

علاء قال: "لَوْ سمحْت، متْقولْش لِحدّ إنيّ قُلْتِلك. أنا بعْزِف جيتار و هشْتغِل في السِّرّ في أيّ حفْلة."

المُدرِّس قال: "ياه؟ بِتِعْرف تِعْزِف جيتار بِجدّ؟ طيِّب، أيْه رأيَك تِعْزِف في حفْل تخرُّج جامْعي؟ و بِالفِلوس دي تِروح الرِّحْلِتيْن!"

"ماشي بسّ لَوْ سمحْت محدِّش يِعْرف."

المُدرِّس قال: "تمام."

لمّا رِجِع علاء لِلبيْت، فِضِل يِتْمرّن و يِعْزِف علشان يِكون أحْسن.

و بعْد ساعات و ساعات مِن التّمْرين نام علاء.

[11:56]

❖ ❖ ❖

The next day, Alaa went to the trip supervisor.

Alaa asked, "Excuse me, sir, I want to go on both trips—the stadium and the desert. Is that possible?"

The teacher replied, "Alright, but that's going to be expensive for you."

Alaa said, "Please, don't tell anyone I told you. I play guitar and I'll secretly work a gig at a party."

The teacher said, "Really? You can actually play guitar? Alright, how about performing at a university graduation party? And with that money, you can go on both trips!"

"Okay, but please—no one can know."

The teacher said, "Alright, deal."

When Alaa got home, he kept practicing and playing so he could be at his best.

And after hours and hours of practice, Alaa fell asleep.

و لمّا صِحي، نِزِل بالجِّيتار الصُّبْح بدْري، و رِكِب تاكْسي و راح المدْرسة.

و بعْد ما وِصِل المدْرسة اتّصل على باباه.

علاء قال: "معْلِشّ يا بابا، احْتِمال أتْأخّر النّهارْده. هكون معَ صُحابي."

الأبّ قال: "خلّي بالك مِن نفْسك!"

علاء كان مبْسوط جدّاً، و كان مبْسوط أكْتر بالجِّيتار. و لمّا راح حفْل التّخرُّج، و عزف كُوَيِّس و الكُل كان مبْسوط مِنُّه. كان الجيتار الحاجة الوَحيدة اللي مبيْكونْش مكْسوف مِنْها.

علاء كان مبْسوط مِن عزْفُه، و خد الفِلوس، و رِجِع البيْت.

⟡ ⟡ ⟡

و تاني يوْم، راح علاء الإسْتاد معَ صُحابُه و فِضِل يِفكّر هَيعْمِل أيْه لمّا يِكون معَ رنا و فيه عدد أقلّ مِن النّاس في الباص.

و لمّا وِصْلوا الإسْتاد بصّ على لوْحِة الأنْدية و شاف إسْم النّادي (RA). إفْتكر رنا على طول. و علشان كِده قرّر يِشجّع النّادي ده معاهُم عشان إسْم رنا.

[13:05]

✧   ✧   ✧

When he woke up, he went out early in the morning with his guitar, took a taxi, and headed to school.

After he arrived at school, Alaa called his dad.

Alaa said, "Sorry, Dad, I might be late today. I'll be with my friends."

His father said, "Take care of yourself!"

Alaa was very happy, and even happier with his guitar. When he went to the graduation party, he played well, and everyone enjoyed it. The guitar was the one thing he never felt embarrassed about.

Alaa was happy with his performance, took the money, and went home.

✧   ✧   ✧

The next day, Alaa went to the stadium with his friends and kept thinking about what he'd do when he's with Rana and there are fewer people on the bus.

When they arrived at the stadium, he looked at the team board and saw the club name (RA). He immediately thought of Rana. So he decided to support that team with them—because of her name.

و وَقْت ما كان علاء سرْحان، أصْحاب علاء صوَّتوا: "جوووووْن! جووووْن!"

أحْمد كمان صوَّت: "شُفْت؟ شُفْت الجوْن؟!"

علاء اِبْتسم و قال: "أيْوَه، جميل!" و بدأ يِصفّق.

و كمَّل سرحانُه[1]، و فِضِل صُحابه يِتْكلَّموا عن الجوْن.

علاء رِجِع البيْت أخيراً بعْد يوْم مُرْهِق، لكنُّه اِتْبسط.

❖ ❖ ❖

أمّا بقى في بيْت رنا، موبايْل رنا بيِرْنّ...

رنا ردِّت: "ألوْ؟"

اللي بيِكلِّمْها قال: "أهْلاً! حضْرِتِك نِسيتي الجيتار بِتاعِك. أقْدر أجيبْهولِك
إزّاي؟"

رنا اِسْتغْربِت و قالِت: "بسّ أنا معنْديش جيتار."

اللي بيِكلِّمْها ردّ: "بسّ ده رقمِك اللي مكْتوب عليْه."

"خلاص تمام." و إدِّتُه العِنْوان.

[14:31]

While Alaa was daydreaming, his friends shouted, "Goooooal! Goooooal!"

Ahmad also shouted, "Did you see that? Did you see the goal?!"

Alaa smiled and said, "Yeah, beautiful!" and started clapping.

And Alaa kept daydreaming, while his friends went on talking about the goal.

Alaa finally got home after a tiring day, but he was happy.

❖   ❖   ❖

Meanwhile, at Rana's house, Rana's phone was ringing...

Rana answered, "Hello?"

The person on the phone said, "Hi! You forgot your guitar. How can I return it to you?"

Rana was confused and said, "But I don't have a guitar."

The caller replied, "But this is your number written on it."

"Alright then," and she gave him the address.

---

[1] Note that سرْحان is the (active participle) adjective *daydreaming*; سرحان is the verbal noun (masdar).

بِاللّيْل، و بعْد ما الرّاجِل جاب الجيتار، أبو رنا سألْها: "أيْه يا رنا الجيتار ده؟"

رنا قالِت: "كان نِفْسي فيه يا بابا و واحْدة صاحْبتي جابِتْهولي شُوَيّة."

أبوها قال: "خلّي بالِك مِنُّه بقى و إوْعي تِبوظيه."

بعْد ما الأبّ نامِ، قفلِت رنا الباب و فضْلِت تِتْفرّج على الجيتار و تِحاوِل تِلْعب بيه، لكِن مكانِتْش بتِعْرف تِلْعب بالجّيتار.

❖   ❖   ❖

عدِّت اللّيالي، و جِه معاد الرِّحْلة للصّحْرا.

طِلِع علاء الأُتوبيس. و اِتْفاجِئ بِالجّيتار اللي شبهْ الجيتار بتاعُه بالظّبْط، و كان معَ رنا و اِتْبسم.

فِضْلِت رنا تِحاوِل تِلْعب عليْه طول الطّريق. لكِن مكانِتْش بتِعْرف تِلْعب عليْه.

علاء قاعِد يِقول لِنفْسُه: "يَلّا قوم كلِّمْها. يَلّا بقى دي دي فُرْصتك!"

"دي الحاجة الوَحيدة اللي هتْساعْدك تِكلِّمْها."

[15:39]

That night, after the man brought the guitar, Rana's father asked her, "What's this guitar, Rana?"

Rana said, "I always wanted one, Dad, and a friend gave it to me for a bit."

Her dad said, "Take good care of it and don't you dare break it."

After her father went to sleep, Rana closed the door and kept looking at the guitar and trying to play it—but she didn't know how to play guitar.

❖   ❖   ❖

The nights passed, and the day of the desert trip finally came.

Alaa got on the bus and was surprised to see a guitar that looked exactly like his, and it was with Rana—he smiled.

Rana kept trying to play it the whole way, but she didn't know how to play.

Alaa kept telling himself, "Come on, go talk to her. This is your chance!"

"This is the one thing that'll help you start a conversation with her."

علاء فِضِل مِحْتار و قال لِنَفْسُه: "أكَلِّمْها؟ مكَلِّمْهاش؟ أكَلِّمْها؟ مكَلِّمْهاش؟ طيِّب إفْرِض أحْرِجْتْني... طيِّب إفْرِض إنّ دي الفُرْصة الوَحيدة!"

و فجْأة الأُتوبيس وِقِف بِسبب مطبّ، فا قام علاء مِن غير قصْد مِن على الكُرْسي و وِقِف شُوَيَّة و بعْدين قرّب لِرنا. و قالّها: "على فِكْرة عنْدي جيتار. و مُمْكِن أساعْدِك."

اِتْبَسِمِت رنا و اِتْبَسِم علاء. و لمّا بدأ علاء يِعلِّمْها لمح الرّقْم اللي مكْتوب على الجيتار و اِتْأكِّد إنّ ده الجيتار بِتاعُه هُوَّ.

لكِنُّه فِضِل يِعلِّمْها و مرْضيش يِقولّها.

علاء سألْها: "حبّيْتي الجيتار؟"

رنا ردِّت: "أَيْوَه، عجبْني أوي، خُصوصاً بعْد ما علِّمْتِني عليْه. ميرْسي[1]!"

اِتْبَسِم علاء.

فِضِل علاء و رنا يِتْكلِّموا، و باقي الوِلاد بيْبُصّوا ليهُم. و البنات اللي كان عددْهُم أكْتر بِكْتير مِن الوِلاد بيْبُصّوا ليهُم برْضُه.

أغْلب الوَقْت مكانْش فيه كلام مُباشِر. لكِن بعْد ساعات وَصل الأُتوبيس لِلواحة اللي في وِسْط الصّحرا. و حَواليْها نخْل و شجر. و كإنّها حِتّة مِن الجنّة.

[16:51]

Alaa stayed unsure and said to himself, "Should I talk to her? Should I not? Talk to her? Don't talk to her? What if I embarrass myself... but what if this is my only chance!"

Suddenly, the bus stopped because of a bump, and Alaa unintentionally got up from his seat, stood for a moment, then walked over to Rana and said, "By the way, I have a guitar. I can help you."

Rana smiled, and so did Alaa. When Alaa started teaching her, he noticed the number written on the guitar and realized it was his.

But he kept teaching her and chose not to tell her.

Alaa asked her, "Do you like the guitar?"

Rana replied, "Yeah, I really like it—especially after you taught me. Thanks!"

Alaa smiled.

Alaa and Rana kept talking while the other boys were looking at them. And the girls—who were way more in number than the boys—were looking too.

Most of the time there weren't many direct words. But after hours, the bus arrived at the oasis in the middle of the desert, surrounded by palm trees and greenery—it was like a piece of paradise.

---

[1] ميرْسِي from French merci

نِزِل المُدَرِّسين و المُشْرِفين بِتوع الرِّحْلة و نصبوا الخِيام. و جهّزوا الخَشب عشان يوَلّعوه و ينوّروا بيه بِاللّيْل.

٭ ٭ ٭

علاء كان دايْماً معَ رنا أَوْ باصِص على رنا و فِضِل يِعلِّمْها العزْف على الجيتار بِتاعُه. مِن غيْر ما يِعرّفْها إنُّه الجيتار بِتاعُه.

رنا بصّت لِعلاء و سألِتُه: "تِفْتِكِر يا علاء إزّاي الجيتار ده وَصل لِيّا؟ و ليْه رقمي مكْتوب عليْه؟"

علاء و هُوَّ بِيِضْحك قال: "تلاقيه بابا نُويل!"

و رنا ضِحْكِت معاه.

علاء قالّها: "أنا هروح شُوَيّة و أرْجعْلك. اِسْتنّيني."

"حاضِر."

راح علاء و هُوَّ بِيِجْري ناحْيِةْ الشّجر و النّخْل و لقى شجرةْ تُفّاح مِن ضِمن مزْرعِةْ الواحة.

علاء طِلع على الشّجرة، و قرّب لِأكْبر تُفّاحة و حفر علامةْ قلْب على التُّفّاحة مِن برّه.

[18:33]

The teachers and trip supervisors got off and set up the tents. They prepared the wood to light a fire to use at night.

❖   ❖   ❖

Alaa was always with Rana or watching her and kept teaching her how to play the guitar—without telling her it was his guitar.

Rana looked at Alaa and asked, "Do you think, Alaa, how did this guitar even get to me? And why is my number written on it?"

Alaa laughed and said, "Maybe it was Santa Claus!"

And Rana laughed with him.

Alaa said to her, "I'm going to go for a bit and I'll come back to you. Wait for me."

"Okay."

Alaa ran toward the trees and palm groves and found an apple tree as part of the oasis farm.

Alaa climbed the tree, got close to the biggest apple, and carved a heart symbol on it.

و رِجِع علاء لِرنا بِسُرْعة و خدْها لِلشّجرة.

رنا سألِت: "فيه أيْه بسّ؟ مالك؟"

علاء فِضِل يِشِدّها مِن إيديْها و يِقول: "هتْشوفي هتْشوفي!"

و لمّا وَصلوا لِشجرةِ التُّفّاح، بصّ علاء لِعيْنيْها و قال: "أنا مُتردِّد و مكْسوف و دي طريقْتي الوَحيدة اللي أقولِّك بيها."

"تقول أيْه؟"

"هِزّي الشّجرة دي كِده."

"بسّ أنا ضعيفة، مقْدرْش."

"يَلّا أنا هساعْدِك."

رنا حرّكِت جِذْع الشّجرة، فا وقْعِت التُّفّاحة اللي مَحْفور عليْها قلْب.

علاء اتْكسف. "أنا..."

و شاوِر على التُّفّاحة مِن ناحْيِةْ القلْب.

رنا حطِّت إيديْها على بُقّها و اِتْكسفِت و خدِت التُّفّاحة مِنُّه، و مِشْيِت و هِيَّ مكْسوفة.

[19:46]

Alaa quickly returned to Rana and took her to the tree.

Rana asked, "What's going on? What's wrong?"

Alaa kept pulling her by the hand, saying, "You'll see, you'll see!"

When they reached the apple tree, Alaa looked into her eyes and said, "I'm hesitant and shy, and this is the only way I can tell you."

"Tell me what?"

"Shake this tree a little."

"But I'm weak, I can't."

"Come on, I'll help you."

Rana shook the tree trunk, and the apple with the carved heart fell.

Alaa got shy. "I..."

And he pointed to the heart on the apple.

Rana put her hand over her mouth, blushed, took the apple from him, and walked away shyly.

بِاللّيْل وَلّع المُدرِّسين في الخشب عشان يِعْمِلوا نار و التّلاميذ قعدوا حَوالينْ النّار دي و معاهُم المُدرِّسين.

المُشْرِف قال: "يا جماعة، أنا لقيْت رنا بِتِعْزِف النّهارْده و لازِم تِعْزِف دِلْوَقْتي و تِبْسِطْنا... يَلّا يا رنا! يَلّا سمّعينا!"

التّلاميذ قالوا بِصوْت واحِد[1]: "يَلّا! يَلّا!"

رنا ضِحْكِت و قالِت: "بلاش يا جماعة، بدل ما يِطْلعْلنا تِعْبان."

المُدرِّس قال: "تِعْبان أيْه بسّ؟ متِقْلقيش، يَلّا بقى اِعْزِفي."

قامِت رنا و هِيّ مكْسوفة و حطّت الجيتار على رِجْلها، و جنْبها علاء، و جنْبهُم أصْحابهُم و المُدرِّسين.

و بدأِت رنا تِعْزِف و التّلاميذ و المُدرِّسين يِصقّفوا... لِحدّ ما فجْأه و هِيّ بِتِعْزِف، سمْعوا صوْت تِعْبان!

فيه بنات صرّخت، و فيه وِلاد جِرْيوا، و فيه اللي مقْدِرْش يِمْشي أساساً مِن الخوْف.

رنا فِضْلِت مُغمّضة عينيْها و بِتِترْعِش.

❖   ❖   ❖

At night, the teachers lit the firewood to make a bonfire, and the students sat around the fire with the teachers.

The supervisor said, "Everyone, I saw Rana playing guitar today, and she has to play for us now and cheer us up... Come on, Rana! Let's hear it!"

The students all shouted, "Come on! Come on!"

Rana laughed and said, "No, guys, let's not—what if a snake comes out?"

The teacher said, "A snake? Don't worry. Come on now, play!"

Rana stood up shyly and placed the guitar on her lap. Next to her was Alaa, and beside them were their friends and the teachers.

Rana started playing, and the students and teachers clapped... until suddenly, while she was playing, they heard the sound of a snake!

Some girls screamed, some boys ran, and others couldn't even move from fear.

Rana kept her eyes shut tight and was trembling.

---

[1] بِصوْت واحِد lit. *in one voice*

قام علاء جايِب بِسُرْعة خشبة مِن جنْب النّار.

و فِضِل يمثِّل إنُّه بِيعْزِف لِلتِّعْبان.

التِّعْبان فِضِل يِتْحرّك معَ العصايَة الخشبية اللي علاء حاطِطْها في بُقُّه و بِيْحرّكْها معَ التِّعْبان. و بدأ يِبْعِد شُوَيّة و شُوَيّة عن المكان اللي كانوا فيه.

المُدرِّس جاب سكِّينة و قال: "هُوَّ راح فيْن؟"

رنا قالِت: "معَ علاء! الِحقُه أرْجوك!"

رِجِع علاء و هُوَّ مبْسوط و قال: "لأ لأ، علاء لِحِق نفْسُه."

رنا ضِحْكِت مِن الفرْحة و التّلاميذ صقّفولُه و الولاد بدأوا بالتّصْفير.

أحْمد قال: "هُوَّ أيْه اللي حصل ده؟ إزّاي يَعْني... إزّاي خشبة؟ و بعْديْن بِتِعْزِف بيها؟ إنْتَ غبي يابْني؟"

علاء ردّ: "لأ مِش غبي. عشان التِّعْبان أساساً مبْيِسْمعْش. و لمّا بِيتْحرّك معَ عازِف النّاي بِيتْحرّك عشان حركةِ النّاي نفْسُه، مِش عشان الصّوْت."

بِنْت قالِت: "سيبك سيبك مِنُّه. تِلاقيه غيران مِن إنّك إنْتَ اللي مشّيْت التِّعْبان." التّلاميذ بدأوا يِضْحكوا.

[22:13]

Alaa quickly grabbed a stick from near the fire.

He started pretending to play it like a flute for the snake.

The snake kept moving with the wooden stick that Alaa held in his mouth, swaying it with the snake. Bit by bit, he led it away from where everyone was.

The teacher grabbed a knife and said, "Where did he go?"

Rana said, "With Alaa! Please go help him!"

Alaa came back smiling and said, "No, no, Alaa saved himself."

Rana laughed with joy, and the students applauded him while the boys started whistling.

Ahmad said, "What even just happened? How... I mean, how did a stick work? And you were playing it? Are you stupid, man?"

Alaa replied, "No, I'm not stupid. Snakes don't actually hear. When they move with the flute player, they're following the motion of the flute, not the sound."

A girl said, "Ignore him. He's just jealous that you're the one who got the snake to leave." The students burst out laughing.

قام علاء مع َ رنا و قالَّها: "شُفْتي لمّا قُلْتي فيه تِعْبان جالْنا تِعْبان إزّاي؟ ما تِقولي إنّ حاجة تانْيَة حِلْوَة مَوْجودة برْضُه. مُمْكِن تِتْحقّق هيَّ كمان!"

رنا ضِحْكِت و قالِت: "لأ دي صُدْفة بسّ. و بعْديْن حاجة حِلْوَة زيّ أيْه؟"

علاء قال: "حُبّي."

رنا اِتْكسفِت.

صاحْبِةِ رنا ندهِت عليْهُم و قالِت: "ما تيجوا هِنا يا جماعة! هنِبْدأ حفْلِةْ الشَّوي!"

⁕ ⁕ ⁕

بعْد الأكْل، المُشْرِف قال: "أيْه رأيْكو بقى نِعْمِل مُسابْقِةْ معْلومات عامّة و نِتْسلّي؟!"

التّلاميذ قالوا: "يَلّا يَلّا!"

المُشْرِف قال: "ماشي، بسّ محدِّش يِجاوِب إلّا ما يِرْفع إيدُه الأوّل." و سأل: "أيْه هُوَّ الحَيَوان اللي عنْدُه قلْبيْن؟"

علاء رفع إيدُه.

المُشْرِف قال: "جاوِب يا علاء."

[23:41]

Alaa stood with Rana and said to her, "See? When you said there was a snake, a snake came! So maybe say something nice exists too. Maybe that'll come true as well!"

Rana laughed and said, "No, that was just a coincidence. And anyway, something nice like what?"

Alaa said, "My love."

Rana blushed.

Rana's friend called out to them and said, "Come on over, everyone! We're starting the barbecue party!"

❖   ❖   ❖

After eating, the supervisor said, "So, how about we do a general knowledge quiz for fun?"

The students said, "Yeah! Let's do it!"

The supervisor said, "Alright, but no one can answer unless they raise their hand first." Then he asked, "What animal has two hearts?"

Alaa raised his hand.

The supervisor said, "Go ahead, Alaa."

علاء قال: "أنا يا أُسْتاذ!"

المُشْرِف قالُه: "إنْتَ عنْدك قلْبيْن إزّاي يَعْني؟"

و بصّ على رنا و قال: "أَيْوَه! قول كِده بقى!" و بدأ يِضْحك.

التّلاميذ و المُدرِّسين ضِحْكوا أكْتر.

المُشْرِف قال: "بسّ لأ لأ، الإجابة هِيَّ الإخْطبوط."

التّلاميذ بِتِضْحك تاني.

❖ ❖ ❖

تاني يوْم الأُتوبيس رِجِع لِلمدينة، و الكُلّ مبْسوط و فرْحان، و علاء قاعِد جنْب رنا.

علاء بصّ لِرنا و قالّها: "الرِّحْلة دي أنا محْظوظ بيها."

رنا ردِّت: "و أنا كمان اِتْبسطْت أوي."

اِتْسم علاء و حطّ إيدُه على إيد رنا.

لمّا رنا نامِت قام علاء و جاب وَرق و كتب فيها رسايِل و حطّها في دايْرِةْ الجيتار. و حطّ الجيتار بيْن إيديْن رنا.

[24:52]

Alaa said, "Me, sir!"

The supervisor replied, "What do you mean you have two hearts?"

And he looked at Rana and said, "Yeah! That's what I'm talking about!" and started laughing.

The students and teachers laughed even more.

The supervisor said, "No, no—seriously now, the answer is the octopus."

The students laughed again.

✦   ✦   ✦

The next day, the bus returned to the city, and everyone was happy and cheerful, with Alaa sitting next to Rana.

Alaa looked at Rana and said, "This trip—I feel lucky because of it."

Rana replied, "I really had a great time too."

Alaa smiled and placed his hand over Rana's hand.

When Rana fell asleep, Alaa got up, grabbed some paper, wrote letters, and placed them inside the guitar's sound hole. Then he placed the guitar in Rana's arms.

و لمّا رنا رِجْعِت البيْت و شافِت الوَرق، كانِت كُلّها رسايِل حُبّ... و كانِت رنا مبْسوطة أوي.

و بعْد أيّام... و أسابيع... و شُهور...

و رنا و علاء بِيِتْعلِّموا سَوا على نفْس الجيتار، المُدرِّس راح لِعلاء و سألُه: "علاء، تِحِبّ إنْتَ تِعْزِف في حفْل التّخرُّج؟ وَلّا نِجيب ناس تانْيَة؟"

علاء ردّ و قال: "لأ لأ، يا أُسْتاذ. هعْزِف أنا. بسّ هاخُد الجيتار اللي في المدْرسة وَقْت الحفْلة بسّ."

المُدرِّس قال: "مفيش مُشْكِلة."

اتّفق علاء معَ رنا على إنّهُم هَيِعْزِفوا سَوا و كانوا بِيِعْزِفوا سَوا كِتير... لِحدّ ما جِهْ يوْم حفْل التّخرج.

المُدرِّس قال: "الحقيقة يا جماعة إحْنا اتّفقْنا معَ فرْقة موسيقية جميلة جِدّاً جِدّاً إسْمها RA يَعْني بِبساطة علاء و رنا."

[26:01]

When Rana got home and saw the papers, they were all love letters... and Rana was so happy.

❖ ❖ ❖

And after days... and weeks... and months...

While Rana and Alaa were learning together on the same guitar, the teacher came to Alaa and asked, "Alaa, would you like to perform at the graduation party? Or should we get someone else?"

Alaa replied, "No, no, sir. I'll perform. But I'll only take the school guitar on the day of the event."

The teacher said, "No problem."

Alaa and Rana agreed to perform together and practiced together a lot... until the day of the graduation party came.

❖ ❖ ❖

The teacher said, "Everyone, we've actually arranged for a really wonderful band called RA, which simply stands for Alaa and Rana."

التّلاميذ كُلُّهُم بِيصقّفوا. و دخل علاء و رنا يِعْزِفوا سَوا و كإنّهُم شخْص واحِد، و عزفوا مِن غيْر وَلا غلْطة و كُلّ التّلاميذ كانوا بِيْصقّفوا.

و وِسْط تصْقيف الطُّلّاب افْتكر علاء فريق RA اللي كان شجّعُه لإسْم رنا. و دِلْوَقْتي بيِسْمع نفْس الإسْم و نفْس التّشجْيع، ناقِص بسّ كِلْمِةْ (جوووْن!)

و بعْد العزْف، اِبْتسم علاء، و بصّ لِرنا، و أنْهوا الحفْلة مع َبعْض.

علاء مِشي معَ رنا و قالّها: "رنا، أنا عايِز أعْترِفْلِك بِحاجة."

رنا قالِت "و أنا كمان. بحبّك."

"لأ، أنا اِعْترفْت بحبّي مِن زمان خلاص. فيه حاجة تانْيَة."

"أيْه هِيَّ؟"

"الجيتار ده كان بِتاعي. و كُنْت نِسيتُه لمّا كُنْت في حفْلة عشان أجيب فِلوس الرّحله دي... بسّ لأ لأ، خلّيه معاكي. أنا مبْسوط إنّه ضاع مِنّي و جالِك أساساً."

"أنا محْظوظة بيك."

"إنْتي الحظّ نفْسُه!"

[27:13]

All the students applauded. Alaa and Rana came on stage and played together as if they were one person. They played without a single mistake, and the students were all clapping.

In the middle of the students' applause, Alaa remembered the RA team he had once supported just for Rana's name. And now he was hearing the same name and the same cheering—only missing the word 'Gooooal!'

After the performance, Alaa smiled, looked at Rana, and they ended the event together.

Alaa walked with Rana and said, "Rana, I want to confess something to you."

Rana said, "Me too. I love you."

"No, I confessed my love a long time ago. This is something else."

"What is it?"

"That guitar was mine. I had left it behind at a gig to earn money for this trip... but no, no—keep it. I'm glad it got lost and ended up with you."

"I'm lucky to have you."

"You are luck itself!"

و مشيوا سَوا.

و بدأِت الحفلات و بدأ النّاس يِطْلبوا علاء و رنا مخْصوص. و اِشْتغلوا لِحدّ ما اِشْتروا الجيتار التّاني. و خلّوا الشِّعار بِتاع الجيتارِيْن... رقم موبايْل رنا.

و مِن هِنا بدأِت الفِرْقة الموسيقية RA اللي هتِفْضل رابِط بيْن علاء و رنا طول العُمْر.

[28:37]

And they walked off together.

The gigs started coming, and people began requesting Alaa and Rana by name. They performed until they could afford a second guitar. They made the signature mark on both guitars... Rana's phone number.

And that's how the musical duo RA began—a bond that would forever link Alaa and Rana.

Arabic Text without Tashkeel

For a more authentic reading challenge, read the story without the aid of diacritics (tashkeel) and the parallel English translation.

أتوبيس المدرسة مستني علاء، دايما آخر واحد بيركب الأتوبيس لإنه أقرب واحد للمدرسة.

نزل علاء من بيته و ركب الأتوبيس. و دايما بيحب يقعد على الجنب اليمين علشان يبص على رنا اللي دايما بتقعد ورا سواق الأتوبيس في الشمال.

و فضل علاء ساكت و هادي، و كل التلاميذ بيعملوا دوشة في الأتوبيس... حتى سواق الأتوبيس أوقات بيتضايق و يقولهم: "ما كفاية بقى! بلاش الصوت العالي. أنا راسي وجعتني!"

لما الأتوبيس وصل للمدرسة، و نزل علاء، لقي أحمد بيجري عليه.

"علاء! أخيرا جيت. أنا كنت مستنيك!"

علاء قال: "ليه بس؟ فيه أيه؟"

أحمد رد: "معلش بس أنا تعبان و مش قادر... كح كح!"

"ألف سلامة!"

"لأ لأ لأ، ألف سلامة أيه بس؟ المفروض أنا في الإذاعة المدرسية. و أنا تعبان و مش قادر... كح كح!"

"أنا عمري ما طلعت الإذاعة المدرسية، و خايف أغلط."

"لأ لأ لأ، مش هتغلط، متخافش."

أحمد نادى بصوت عالي: " خلاص يا أستاذ فهمي... علاء هيطلع مكاني!"

"بس أنا مقلتش إني هطلع."

أحمد قال: "خلاص بقى، خليك جدع معايا!"

الأستاذ فهمي راح لعلاء و قاله: "يلا يا علاء! هتقرا الأخبار الصباحية، و خلي صوتك هادي و متقراش بسرعة."

علاء رد: "بس أنا..."

الأستاذ فهمي بصوت عالي زع: "يلا كله على طابوره!"

وقف علاء ماسك الجرنال و بدأ يقرا الخبر بينه و بين نفسه علشان ميتلخبطش.

و علاء اتوتر و بدأ يعرق.

و أحمد واقف في طابور فصله و قاعد يضحك مع صحابه.

علاء قال لنفسه: "مستحيل أحمد يكون تعبان. تعبان و هيضحك و يلعب كده إزاي؟!"

تلميذ نادى من بعيد: "أستاذ فهمي! أستاذ فهمي! المايكرفون مش شغال!"

أستاذ فهمي قال: "يعني أيه مش شغال؟"

بدأت أصوات التلاميذ في الطابور تعلى و بدأ الضحك و الهزار. و الأستاذ فهمي فضل يحاول يصلح المايكرفون.

الأستاذ فهمي قال بصوت عالي: "خلاص دلوقتي! اطلعوا للفصول."

علاء حط الجرنال على الطرابيزة.، و طلع مع أصحابه للفصل و هو متنرفز.

لكن الأستاذ فهمي وقفه. "إنت مرعوب كده ليه؟ خايف من شوية كلام هتقولهم في المايكرفون؟"

علاء رد: "هو أنا بس..."

"اطلع خلاص، أنا بنصحك!"

طلع علاء للفصل و هو متضايق و شاف أحمد.

علاء زعق لأحمد و قال: "مكانش ينفع تعمل اللي إنت عملته ده على فكرة!"

"يا عم خلاص بقى محصلش حاجة."

"لأ حصل! إنت خليتني متضايق دلوقتي."

دخل المدرس على التلاميذ و قالهم: "سكوت! سكوت!"

و بعدين كمل: "بما إني جديد هنا، فا عرفوني بيكم يا شباب! أنا أستاذ اللغة العربية و إن شاء الله يكون درس ممتع ليكو. النهارده مش هناخد حاجات كتير. كل واحد بس يكتب بياناته في ورقة علشان أقدر أتواصل مع أهلكو دايما!"

الطلاب كتبوا البيانات: الإسم، رقم التليفون، و رقم الفصل.

علاء كان دايما بيقعد في أول كرسي. و علشان كده المدرس قاله يلم الورق و يوديهوله على المكتب.

علاء كان بيلم الورق من الطلاب... و لما خد الورقة بتاعة رنا، خلى الورقة بتاعتها آخر ورقة.

و بعد ما لم كل الورق، و هو رايح للمدرس، شاف ورقة رنا. و فضل يردد رقم التليفون كإنه بيردد الأخبار بتاعة الجرنال بالظبط.

بعد ما وصل الورق للمدرس، راح الحمام و كتب بسرعة على إيده رقم رنا. بس من تحت كم القميص اللي كان لابسه عشان محدش يشوفه.

و لما طلع علاء من الحمام، شاف الأستاذ فهمي.

علاء قال: "يا أستاذ فهمي، ممكن تديني فرصة أثبتلك إني شجاع؟"

الأستاذ فهمي رد و قال: "الإثبات هو إثبات لنفسك، مش ليا!"

"طيب، ممكن أعزف بكره في طابور المدرسة... بالجيتار بتاعي؟"

"ماشي، و متخافش تاني بعد كده!"

بعد أول يوم دراسي، رجع علاء في الأتوبيس... و لإنه آخر واحد بيركب الأتوبيس، إلا إنه أول واحد بينزل من الأتوبيس.

علاء قال لنفسه و هو باصص على رنا: "مكتوب عليا أشوفك دقايق قبل ما أنزل و دقايق بعد ما أركب. لو كان في إيدي، كنت هخليكي قدامي كده ٢٤ ساعة!"

رنا كانت متوسطة الجمال. على غير المتوقع علاء كمان كان متوسط الجمال، لكنه كان شايف إن رنا أجمل بنت في الفصل كله.

نزل علاء من الأتوبيس و رجع البيت.

لما رجع علاء البيت و بعد ساعات، اتصل على رقم رنا.

و قلب علاء بينبض بقوة و بيتحرك من مكانه... لحد ما رنا ردت: "ألو؟"

علاء حط إيده على بقه عشان صوته ميطلعش. و فضل يسمع رنا و هي بتقول: "ألو؟ ألو؟" لحد ما قفلت المكالمة.

دخل علاء أوضته و هو مبسوط، و جاب الجيتار بتاعه، و قفل باب الأوضة، و قعد يعزف و يرقص بالجيتار بتاعه. "ألو! ألو! ألووووو! ألو!"

و كتب رقم رنا على ضهر الجيتار و رسم جنبه قلب و حط الجيتار جنبه على السرير.

❖   ❖   ❖

تاني يوم راح علاء بسرعة و جاب الجيتار اللي في أوضة الموسيقى و جهز نفسه قبل الطابور كله ما يبدأ.

الأستاذ فهمي بص لعلاء و قاله: "جاهز يا علاء؟"

علاء شاور براسه لتحت: "أيوه."

و لما بدأ الطابور و بدأ علاء العزف، بدأ واثق من نفسه لكنه بص لرنا في الطابور.

و حس إنه بدأ يتلخبط. و بعد عشر دقايق حس إن أصوات كلام التلاميذ أعلى من صوت العزف بتاعه.

و بص لرنا تاني و اتوتر أكتر و قام فجأه و وقف عزف.

و التلاميذ ضحكوا بصوت عالي و أولهم أحمد. و الأستاذ فهمي قال بصوت متنرفز: "اطلعوا للفصل!"

❖ ❖ ❖

التلاميذ و هما داخلين الفصل فضلوا يضحكوا.

أحمد قال لعلاء بتريقة: "أيه العزف ده كله يا فنان؟"

علاء رد: "إني أعزف وحش أحسن من إنك مبتعزفش خالص على فكرة." قام مشي أحمد.

فضل علاء باصص ناحية البنات... لرنا بمعنى أصح.

المدرس دخل و بص علاء للمدرس، و كل مرة المدرس يكتب على السبورة، يستغل علاء اللحظات دي في إنه يبص لرنا. مستني منها تبصله مرة واحدة، و لو بالصدفة.

المدرس بص للتلاميذ و قالهم: "درس النهارده عن العطاء!"

و بعد شرح كتير خلص الدرس، و خلصت كل الدروس و التلاميذ رجعوا للبيت. و رجع علاء للبيت و فضل يتصل تاني و تاني برنا. عشان بس يسمع "ألو؟" و أحيانا "مين معايا؟"

أبو علاء دخل على علاء الأوضة، قام علاء قافل التليفون بسرعة.

أبو علاء قال: "بيقولوا فيه رحلة للصحرا مع المدرسة. عايز تروح؟"

"لأ بلاش. هنا أحسن من الصحرا. و بعدين فيه رحلة للإستاد ممكن أروحها مع صحابي."

"خلاص ماشي، شوف إنت عايز أيه."

جرس التليفون رن.

أبو علاء قال: "روح بقى رد بسرعة. تلاقيهم أصحابك."

رد علاء على التليفون، و قال: "ألو، مين معايا؟"

"أنا صاحبك يا عمر. قول بس، هتيجي معانا الإستاد و نشوف ماتش كورة ولا تروح رحلة الصحرا مع البنات؟"

"هو كل اللي رايح الصحرا بنات بس يعني؟"

واحد تاني من الصحاب قال: "هههههه لأ لأ. بس عشان إحنا رجالة نروح أحسن الإستاد."

"أنا قلت لبابا فعلا بلاش فكرة الصحرا دي."

واحد من صحاب علاء قال: "خلاص اتفقنا. الإستاد إن شاء الله!"

❖ ❖ ❖

بعدها بيوم علاء راح لمشرف الرحلات.

علاء سأل: "لو سمحت يا أستاذ، أنا عايز أروح الرحلتين. الإستاد و الصحرا. ممكن؟"

المدرس رد: "ماشي بس كده هيكون غالي عليك."

علاء قال: "لو سمحت، متقولش لحد إني قلتلك. أنا بعزف جيتار و هشتغل في السر في أي حفلة."

المدرس قال: "ياه؟ بتعرف تعزف جيتار بجد؟ طيب، أيه رأيك تعزف في حفل تخرج جامعي؟ و بالفلوس دي تروح الرحلتين!"

"ماشي بس لو سمحت محدش يعرف."

المدرس قال: "تمام."

لما رجع علاء للبيت، فضل يتمرن و يعزف علشان يكون أحسن.

و بعد ساعات و ساعات من التمرين نام علاء.

❖   ❖   ❖

و لما صحي، نزل بالجيتار الصبح بدري، و ركب تاكسي و راح المدرسة.

و بعد ما وصل المدرسة اتصل على باباه.

علاء قال: "معلش يا بابا، احتمال أتأخر النهارده. هكون مع صحابي."

الأب قال: "خلي بالك من نفسك!"

علاء كان مبسوط جدا، و كان مبسوط أكتر بالجيتار. و لما راح حفل التخرج، و عزف كويس و الكل كان مبسوط منه. كان الجيتار الحاجة الوحيدة اللي مبيكونش مكسوف منها.

علاء كان مبسوط من عزفه، و خد الفلوس، و رجع البيت.

❖   ❖   ❖

و تاني يوم، راح علاء الإستاد مع صحابه و فضل يفكر هيعمل أيه لما يكون مع رنا و فيه عدد أقل من الناس في الباص.

و لما وصلوا الإستاد بص على لوحة الأندية و شاف إسم النادي (RA). إفتكر رنا على طول.

و علشان كده قرر يشجع النادي ده معاهم عشان إسم رنا.

و وقت ما كان علاء سرحان، أصحاب علاء صوتوا: "جوووووون! جووون!"

أحمد كمان صوت: "شفت؟ شفت الجون؟!"

علاء ابتسم و قال: "أيوه، جميل!" و بدأ يصقف.

و كمل سرحانه، و فضل صحابه يتكلموا عن الجون.

علاء رجع البيت أخيرا بعد يوم مرهق، لكنه اتبسط.

❖   ❖   ❖

أما بقى في بيت رنا، موبايل رنا بيرن...

رنا ردت: "ألو؟"

اللي بيكلمها قال: "أهلا! حضرتك نسيتي الجيتار بتاعك. أقدر أجيبهولك إزاي؟"

رنا استغربت و قالت: "بس أنا معنديش جيتار."

اللي بيكلمها رد: "بس ده رقمك اللي مكتوب عليه."

"خلاص تمام." و إدته العنوان.

بالليل، و بعد ما الراجل جاب الجيتار، أبو رنا سألها: "أيه يا رنا الجيتار ده؟"

رنا قالت: "كان نفسي فيه يا بابا و واحدة صاحبتي جابتهولي شوية."

أبوها قال: "خلي بالك منه بقى و إوعي تبوظيه."

بعد ما الأب نام، قفلت رنا الباب و فضلت تتفرج على الجيتار و تحاول تلعب بيه، لكن مكانتش بتعرف تلعب بالجيتار.

❖   ❖   ❖

عدت الليالي، و جه معاد الرحلة للصحرا.

طلع علاء الأتوبيس. و اتفاجئ بالجيتار اللي شبه الجيتار بتاعه بالظبط، و كان مع رنا و ابتسم.

فضلت رنا تحاول تلعب عليه طول الطريق. لكن مكانتش بتعرف تلعب عليه.

علاء قاعد يقول لنفسه: "يلا قوم كلمها. يلا بقى دي فرصتك!"

"دي الحاجة الوحيدة اللي هتساعدك تكلمها."

علاء فضل محتار و قال لنفسه: "أكلمها؟ مكلمهاش؟ أكلمها؟ مكلمهاش؟ طيب إفرض أحرجتني... طيب إفرض إن دي الفرصة الوحيدة!"

و فجأة الأتوبيس وقف بسبب مطب، فا قام علاء من غير قصد من على الكرسي و وقف شوية و بعدين قرب لرنا. و قالها: "على فكرة عندي جيتار. و ممكن أساعدك."

ابتسمت رنا و ابتسم علاء. و لما بدأ علاء يعلمها لمح الرقم اللي مكتوب على الجيتار و اتأكد إن ده الجيتار بتاعه هو.

لكنه فضل يعلمها و مرضيش يقولها.

علاء سألها: "حبيتي الجيتار؟"

رنا ردت: "أيوه، عجبني أوي، خصوصا بعد ما علمتني عليه. ميرسي!"

ابتسم علاء.

فضل علاء و رنا يتكلموا، و باقي الولاد بيبصوا ليهم. و البنات اللي كان عددهم أكتر بكتير من الولاد بيبصوا ليهم برضه.

أغلب الوقت مكانش فيه كلام مباشر. لكن بعد ساعات وصل الأتوبيس للواحة اللي في وسط الصحرا. و حواليها نخل و شجر. و كإنها حتة من الجنة.

نزل المدرسين و المشرفين بتوع الرحلة و نصبوا الخيام. و جهزوا الخشب عشان يولعوه و ينوروا بيه بالليل.

✧ ✧ ✧

علاء كان دايما مع رنا أو باصص على رنا و فضل يعلمها العزف على الجيتار بتاعه. من غير ما يعرفها إنه الجيتار بتاعه.

رنا بصت لعلاء و سألته: "تفتكر يا علاء إزاي الجيتار ده وصل ليا؟ و ليه رقمي مكتوب عليه؟"

علاء و هو بيضحك قال: "تلاقيه بابا نويل!"

و رنا ضحكت معاه.

علاء قالها: "أنا هروح شوية و أرجعلك. استنيني."

"حاضر."

راح علاء و هو بيجري ناحية الشجر و النخل و لقى شجرة تفاح من ضمن مزرعة الواحة.

علاء طلع على الشجرة، و قرب لأكبر تفاحة و حفر علامة قلب على التفاحة من بره.

و رجع علاء لرنا بسرعة و خدها للشجرة.

رنا سألت: "فيه أيه بس؟ مالك؟"

علاء فضل يشدها من إيديها و يقول: "هتشوفي هتشوفي!"

و لما وصلوا لشجرة التفاح، بص علاء لعينيها و قال: "أنا متردد و مكسوف و دي طريقتي الوحيدة اللي أقولك بيها."

"تقول أيه؟"

"هزي الشجرة دي كده."

"بس أنا ضعيفة، مقدرش."

"يلا أنا هساعدك."

رنا حركت جذع الشجرة، فا وقعت التفاحة اللي محفور عليها قلب.

علاء اتكسف. "أنا..."

و شاور على التفاحة من ناحية القلب.

رنا حطت إيديها على بقها و اتكسفت و خدت التفاحة منه، و مشيت و هي مكسوفة.

❖ ❖ ❖

بالليل ولع المدرسين في الخشب عشان يعملوا نار و التلاميذ قعدوا حوالين النار دي و معاهم المدرسين.

المشرف قال: "يا جماعة، أنا لقيت رنا بتعزف النهارده و لازم تعزف دلوقتي و تبسطنا... يلا يا رنا! يلا سمعينا!"

التلاميذ قالوا بصوت واحد: "يلا! يلا!"

رنا ضحكت و قالت: "بلاش يا جماعة، بدل ما يطلعلنا تعبان."

المدرس قال: "تعبان أيه بس؟ متقلقيش، يلا بقى اعزفي."

قامت رنا و هي مكسوفة و حطت الجيتار على رجلها. و جنبها علاء، و جنبهم أصحابهم و المدرسين.

و بدأت رنا تعزف و التلاميذ و المدرسين يصقفوا... لحد ما فجأه و هي بتعزف، سمعوا صوت تعبان!

فيه بنات صرخت، و فيه ولاد جريوا، و فيه اللي مقدرش يمشي أساسا من الخوف.

رنا فضلت مغمضة عينيها و بتترعش.

قام علاء جايب بسرعة خشبة من جنب النار.

و فضل يمثل إنه بيعزف للتعبان.

التعبان فضل يتحرك مع العصاية الخشبية اللي علاء حاططها في بقه و بيحركها مع التعبان. و بدأ يبعد شوية و شوية عن المكان اللي كانوا فيه.

المدرس جاب سكينة و قال: "هو راح فين؟"

رنا قالت: "مع علاء! الحقه أرجوك!"

رجع علاء و هو مبسوط و قال: "لأ لأ، علاء لحق نفسه."

رنا ضحكت من الفرحة و التلاميذ صقفوله و الولاد بدأوا بالتصفير.

أحمد قال: "هو أيه اللي حصل ده؟ إزاي يعني... إزاي خشبة؟ و بعدين بتعزف بيها؟ إنت غبي يابني؟"

علاء رد: "لأ مش غبي. عشان التعبان أساسا مبيسمعش. و لما بيتحرك مع عازف الناي بيتحرك عشان حركة الناي نفسه، مش عشان الصوت."

بنت قالت: "سيبك سيبك منه. تلاقيه غيران من إنك إنت اللي مشيت التعبان." التلاميذ بدأوا يضحكوا.

قام علاء مع رنا و قالها: "شفتي لما قلتي فيه تعبان جالنا تعبان إزاي؟ ما تقولي إن حاجة تانية حلوة موجودة برضه. ممكن تتحقق هي كمان!"

رنا ضحكت و قالت: "لأ دي صدفة بس. و بعدين حاجة حلوة زي أيه؟"

علاء قال: "حبي."

رنا اتكسفت.

صاحبة رنا ندهت عليهم و قالت: "ما تيجوا هنا يا جماعة! هنبدأ حفلة الشوي!"

❖ ❖ ❖

بعد الأكل، المشرف قال: "أيه رأيكو بقى نعمل مسابقة معلومات عامة و نتسلي؟!"

التلاميذ قالوا: "يلا يلا!"

المشرف قال: "ماشي، بس محدش يجاوب إلا ما يرفع إيده الأول." و سأل: "أيه هو الحيوان اللي عنده قلبين؟"

علاء رفع إيده.

المشرف قال: "جاوب يا علاء."

علاء قال: "أنا يا أستاذ."

المشرف قاله: "إنت عندك قلبين إزاي يعني؟"

و بص على رنا و قال: "أيوه! قول كده بقى!" و بدأ يضحك.

التلاميذ و المدرسين ضحكوا أكتر.

المشرف قال: "بس لأ لأ، الإجابة هي الإخطبوط."

التلاميذ بتضحك تاني.

❖   ❖   ❖

تاني يوم الأتوبيس رجع للمدينة، و الكل مبسوط و فرحان، و علاء قاعد جنب رنا.

علاء بص لرنا و قالها: "الرحلة دي أنا محظوظ بيها."

رنا ردت: "و أنا كمان اتبسطت أوي."

ابتسم علاء و حط إيده على إيد رنا.

لما رنا نامت قام علاء و جاب ورق و كتب فيها رسايل و حطها في دايرة الجيتار. و حط الجيتار بين إيدين رنا.

و لما رنا رجعت البيت و شافت الورق، كانت كلها رسايل حب... و كانت رنا مبسوطة أوي.

❖   ❖   ❖

و بعد أيام... و أسابيع... و شهور...

و رنا و علاء بيتعلموا سوا على نفس الجيتار، المدرس راح لعلاء و سأله: "علاء، تحب إنت تعزف في حفل التخرج؟ ولا نجيب ناس تانية؟"

علاء رد و قال: "لأ لأ، يا أستاذ. هعزف أنا. بس هاخد الجيتار اللي في المدرسة وقت الحفلة بس."

المدرس قال: "مفيش مشكلة."

اتفق علاء مع رنا على إنهم هيعزفوا سوا و كانوا بيعزفوا سوا كتير... لحد ما جه يوم حفل التخرج.

❖   ❖   ❖

المدرس قال: "الحقيقة يا جماعة إحنا اتفقنا مع فرقة موسيقية جميلة جدا جدا إسمها RA يعني ببساطة علاء و رنا.

التلاميذ كلهم بيصقفوا.

و دخل علاء و رنا يعزفوا سوا و كإنهم شخص واحد، و عزفوا من غير ولا غلطة و كل التلاميذ كانوا بيصقفوا.

و وسط تصقيف الطلاب افتكر علاء فريق RA اللي كان شجعه لإسم رنا. و دلوقتي بيسمع نفس الإسم و نفس التشجيع، ناقص بس كلمة (جووون!)

و بعد العزف، ابتسم علاء، و بص لرنا، و أنهوا الحفلة مع بعض.

علاء مشي مع رنا و قالها: "رنا، أنا عايز أعترفلك بحاجة."

رنا قالت "و أنا كمان. بحبك."

"لأ، أنا اعترفت بحبي من زمان خلاص. فيه حاجة تانية."

"أيه هي؟"

"الجيتار ده كان بتاعي. و كنت نسيته لما كنت في حفلة عشان أجيب فلوس الرحله دي... بس لأ لأ، خليه معاكي. أنا مبسوط إنه ضاع مني و جالك أساسا."

"أنا محظوظة بيك."

"إنتي الحظ نفسه!"

و مشيوا سوا.

و بدأت الحفلات و بدأ الناس يطلبوا علاء و رنا مخصوص. و اشتغلوا لحد ما اشتروا الجيتار التاني. و خلوا الشعار بتاع الجيتارين... رقم موبايل رنا.

و من هنا بدأت الفرقة الموسيقية RA. اللي هتفضل رابط بين علاء و رنا طول العمر.

Comprehension Questions

1. ليه علاء دايماً بيبْقى آخِر واحِد يِركب الأُتوبيس؟

2. أيْه اللي خلّى علاء يِحِبّ يُقْعُد في الجنْب اليمين في الأُتوبيس؟

3. أيْه اللي أحْمد طلبه مِن علاء في أوّل اليوْم؟

4. ليه علاء كان خايِف يِطْلع في الإذاعة المدْرسية؟

5. علاء جاب فِلوس الرِّحْلتيْن مِنيْن؟

6. أيْه سِرّ اِخْتيار علاء لفريق RA في الإسْتاد؟

7. أيْه اللي علاء كتبُه على التُّفّاحة؟

8. إزّاي الجيتار وَصل لرنا؟

9. ليه علاء إخْتار يِسْتخْدِم عصايةٍ خشب معَ التِّعْبان؟

10. أيْه كان تفْسير علاء لما التِّعْبان كان بيِتْحرّك معَ النّاي؟

11. أيْه اللي كان مكْتوب على الوَرق اللي في الجيتار؟

12. إزّاي علاء و رنا اِخْتاروا إسْم فِرْقِتْهُم؟

13. ليه علاء ما قالْش لرنا على الجيتار في الأوّل؟

14. أيْه كان ردّ فِعْل رنا لمّا عِرْفِت إنّ الجيتار كان بِتاع علاء؟

15. علاء كان بيعْمل أيْه لمّا كان بيِتّصِل برنا في الأوّل؟

16. ردّ فِعْل المُدرِّسين كان أيْه على عزْف علاء و رنا في الحفْلة؟

17. إزّاي علاء ساعِد رنا تِتْعلِّم العزْف على الجيتار؟

18. أيْه كان شُعور علاء لمّا شاف الجيتار معَ رنا وهُمّا في رِحْلةٍ الصّحْرا؟

19. ليه علاء كتب رقم رنا على إيدُه؟

20. الشِّعار النِّهائي لِلْفِرْقة الموسيقية كان أيْه؟

1. Why was Alaa always the last one to get on the bus?
2. What made Alaa prefer sitting on the right side of the bus?
3. What did Ahmad ask Alaa to do at the beginning of the day?
4. Why was Alaa afraid to participate in the school broadcast?
5. How did Alaa get money for both trips?
6. What was the secret behind Alaa's choice of team RA at the stadium?
7. What did Alaa carve on the apple?
8. How did the guitar reach Rana?
9. Why did Alaa choose to use a wooden stick with the snake?
10. What was Alaa's explanation for the snake's movement with the flute?
11. What was written on the papers in the guitar?
12. How did Alaa and Rana choose their band's name?
13. Why didn't Alaa tell Rana about the guitar at first?
14. What was Rana's reaction when she learned the guitar was Alaa's?
15. What did Alaa do when he first called Rana?
16. What was the teachers' reaction to Alaa and Rana's performance at the ceremony?
17. How did Alaa help Rana learn to play the guitar?
18. How did Alaa feel when he saw the guitar with Rana on the desert trip?
19. Why did Alaa write Rana's number on his hand?
20. What was the final emblem of the musical band?

Answers to the Comprehension Questions

1. عشان بيتُه كان أقْرب واحِد للْمدْرسة.

2. عشان يِقْدر يبُصّ على رنا اللي بِتُقْعُد وَرا السّوّاق على الشِّمال.

3. طلب مِنُّه إنُّه يطْلع مكانه في الإذاعة المدْرسية عشان هُوَّ تعْبان.

4. عشان هُوَّ مطْلِعْش فيها قبْل كِده و خايف يغْلط.

5. مِن العزْف بالْجيتار في حفْلة تخرُّج في الجامعة.

6. إخْتارُه عشان الحُروف دي بِتْفكّرُه بِإسْم رنا.

7. حفر علىْها شكْل قلْب.

8. علاء نِسيْه في حفْلةِ التّخرُّج و حدّ لقاه و وصّلُه لِرنا بعْد ما لقى رقمْها مكْتوب عليْه.

9. عشان يِقْدر يتْحكّم في حركةِ التِّعْبان و يبْعدُه عن المكان.

10. قال إنّ التّعابين مبْتِسْمعْش وبِتِتحرّك بسّ معَ حركةِ النّاي نفْسُه.

11. كانِت كُلّها رسايِل حُبّ مِن علاء لِرنا.

12. إخْتاروا RA مِن الحُروف الأولى مِن إسْميْهُم (رنا و علاء).

13. عشان يِفْضل يعلّمْها و يكون قُرِيِّب مِنْها.

14. قالِتْلُه إنّها محْظوظة إنّها معاه.

15. كان بِيْحُطّ إيدُه على بُقُّه و مبِيْتكلّمْش، كان بسّ بِيسْمع صوتْها و هيَّ بِتْقول "ألو".

16. كانوا مبْسوطين و فخورين بيهُم و وَصفوهُم بالْفِرْقة الموسيقية الهايْلة.

17. قعد معاها و علّمْها وهُمّا في رِحْلةِ الصّحْرا و بعْدين فِضْلوا يِتْمرّنوا سَوا.

18. كان مبْسوط و اِبْتسم لمّا شافُه معاها.

19. عشان يِحْفظُه و يِتّصِل بيها، و كتبُه تحْت كُمّ القميص عشان محدِّش يِشوفه.

20. رقم تِليفوْن رنا على الجيتاريْن.

1. Because his house was the closest to the school.
2. So he could look at Rana who always sat behind the driver on the left.
3. To take his place in the school broadcast because he was sick.
4. Because he had never participated before and was afraid of making mistakes.
5. By playing guitar at a university graduation ceremony.
6. He chose it because the letters reminded him of Rana's name.
7. He carved a heart shape on it.
8. Alaa forgot it at the graduation ceremony and someone found it and delivered it to Rana after finding her number written on it.
9. To be able to control the snake's movement and guide it away from the area.
10. He explained that snakes can't hear and only move with the physical movement of the flute itself.
11. They were all love letters from Alaa to Rana.
12. They chose RA from the first letters of their names (Rana and Alaa).
13. So he could continue teaching her and get closer to her.
14. She told him she was lucky to have him.
15. He would put his hand over his mouth and not speak, just listening to her voice saying "hello."
16. They were happy and proud of them and described them as a wonderful musical group.
17. He sat with her and taught her during the desert trip and then they continued practicing together.
18. He was happy and smiled when he saw it with her.
19. To memorize it and call her, and he wrote it under his shirt sleeve so no one would see it.
20. Rana's phone number on both guitars.

Summary

Read the scrambled summary of the story below. Write the correct number (1–10) in the blank next to each event to show the proper sequence.

علاء بيرِكب باص المدْرسة و بيحِبّ يشوف رنا.   ــــــ

علاء اِعْترف لِرنا إنّ الجيتار كان بِتاعُه.   ــــــ

وهُمّا في رِحْلةِ الصّحْرا، علاء علّم رنا العزْف و عبّر عن حُبُّه.   ــــــ

أحْمد طلب مِن علاء إنّه يطْلع مكانُه في الإذاعة المدْرسية.   ــــــ

علاء خد رقم رنا مِن وَرقةِ البَيانات و اِتّصل بيها.   ــــــ

علاء راح الإسْتاد و اِخْتار فريق RA عشان إسْم رنا.   ــــــ

رنا لِقْيِت الجيتار بِتاع علاء و حاوْلِت تِتْعلّم عليْه.   ــــــ

علاء و رنا عزفوا سَوا في حفْل التّخرُّج.   ــــــ

علاء عزف في حفْلةِ تخرُّج عشان يجيب فِلوس لِلرِّحْلتيْن.   ــــــ

علاء و رنا عملوا فِرْقةِ RA و اِشْتغلوا سَوا.   ــــــ

Key to the Summary

1   Alaa would ride the school bus and liked to see Rana.

9   Alaa confessed to Rana that the guitar was his.

7   During the desert trip, Alaa taught Rana to play and expressed his love.

2   Ahmad asked Alaa to take his place in the school broadcast.

3   Alaa took Rana's number from the information sheet and called her.

5   Alaa went to the stadium and chose team RA because of Rana's name.

6   Rana found Alaa's guitar and tried to learn on it.

8   Alaa and Rana played together at the graduation ceremony.

4   Alaa played at a graduation ceremony to get money for both trips.

10 Alaa and Rana formed band RA and worked together.

Egyptian Arabic Readers Series

www.lingualism.com/ear

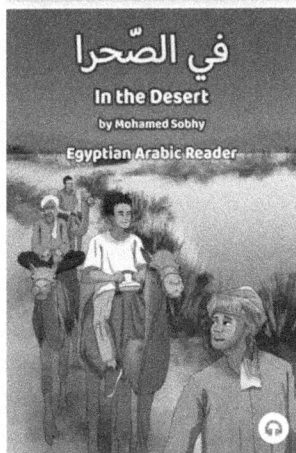

أحْلام صامْتة
Silent Dreams
by Nourhan Sabek
Egyptian Arabic Reader

لعْنة الإسْكنْدر
Alexander's Curse
by Mostafa Abdel Nasser
Egyptian Arabic Reader

Egyptian Arabic Reader
ميدان التّحْرير
Tahrir Square
by Mohamad Osman

في الصّحرا
In the Desert
by Mohamed Sobhy
Egyptian Arabic Reader

Egyptian Arabic Reader
أمل
Hope
by Nourhan Sabek

Egyptian Arabic Reader
الصّداقة ولّا الحبّ؟
Friendship or Love?
by Nourhan Sabek

شيريهان
sherihan
Egyptian Arabic Reader

سرّ النّجاح
The Secret of Success

جنّار الحبّ
The Guitar of Love
Egyptian Arabic Reader
الدّجّال
The Charlatan

كأنّي بنبُص في المراية
Like Looking in a Mirror
Egyptian Arabic Reader

دليل الكلب لمفكّر بنقبل
A Dog's Fate

Egyptian Arabic Reader
جوازي صالوْنات
My Arranged Marriage
by Nourhan Sabek

Egyptian Arabic Reader
الصّيّاد و العمْلة المعْدنية
The Fisherman and the Coin
by Mohamed Sobhy

المومْيا
The Mummy
by Mohamad Osman
Egyptian Arabic Reader

www.ingramcontent.com/pod-product-compliance
Lightning Source LLC
Chambersburg PA
CBHW072051040426
42447CB00012BB/3095

* 9 7 8 1 9 4 9 6 5 0 1 3 6 *